Technology
OF ANCIENT EGYPT

Leslie C. Kaplan

The Rosen Publishing Group's
PowerKids Press™
PRIMARY SOURCE

New York

To Camille

Published in 2004 by The Rosen Publishing Group, Inc.
29 East 21st Street, New York, NY 10010

First Edition

Editors: Rachel O'Connor and John Cassel
Book Design: Maria E. Melendez
Photo Researcher: Adriana Skura

Photo Credits: Cover photo and pp. 7, 19 (inset) © Erich Lessing/Art Resource, NY; cover (inset), p. 20 (top) © Giraudon/Art Resource, NY; p. 4 The Art Archive/Egyptian Museum Cairo/ Dagli Orti; p. 4 (inset) © Roger Wood/CORBIS; pp. 8, 11 (left), 12 The Art Archive/Dagli Orti; pp. 11 (right), 16, 20 (bottom) The Granger Collection, New York; p. 12 (inset) © Werner Forman/Art Resource, NY; p. 15 The Art Archive/Ragab Papyrus Institute Cairo/Dagli Orti; p. 19 © Art Resource, NY; p.20 (center) The Art Archive/Musée du Louvre Paris/Dagli Orti.

Kaplan, Leslie C.
Technology of ancient Egypt / Leslie C. Kaplan.— 1st ed.
    v. cm. — (Primary sources of ancient civilizations. Egypt)
Includes bibliographical references and index.
Contents: An advanced civilization—Tools for building—The great pyramids of Egypt—Using the Nile river—Making strides in transportation—The Egyptian calendar—The invention of clocks—Advances in medicine—Building better weapons—Writing it all down.
    ISBN 0-8239-6785-9—ISBN 0-8239-8934-8 (pbk.)
    1. Technology—Egypt—History—To 332 B.C.—Juvenile literature. 2. Egypt—Civilization—To 332 B.C.—Juvenile literature. [1. Technology—Egypt—History—To 332 B.C. 2. Egypt—Civilization—To 332 B.C.]
I. Title. II. Series.
    T27.3.E3 K37 2004
    609.32—dc21
                                                              2002154510

Manufactured in the United States of America

Contents

The Egyptians built boats to transport the large blocks of stone used for pyramids.

With the invention of sails around 2900 B.C., the ancient Egyptians could transport goods by boat much faster than before, when men had to row using oars, as above.

An Advanced Civilization

The Nile River had a major effect on technology in ancient Egypt. Life in Egypt improved because Egyptians developed inventions that made the best use of the water from the Nile. They made farming tools to help work the rich soil that the river left behind every year after it flooded. They invented their calendar based on this yearly cycle of the river. They came up with an irrigation system to help spread the water from the Nile. They made boats to transport heavy building materials on the river. Ancient Egyptian technology was so advanced that Egyptian inventions, such as pyramids, are still remarkable today.

Tools for Building

Some of the world's most magnificent buildings were built by the Egyptians. With simple tools, the Egyptians changed blocks of stone into majestic pyramids and temples. These tools included picks, drills, and chisels made of copper, bronze, and basalt. Egyptians used the tools to break off large blocks of stone from desert quarries, areas where stone can be found, and to cut the blocks into smaller pieces. The Egyptians made a sled that could carry as much as 2 ½ tons (2.3 t) of rock. As many as 100 men would pull the sled to the boats waiting on the Nile River. The boats transported the slabs of rock to wherever the structure was being built.

This wall painting, found in an ancient Egyptian tomb, shows carpenters at work. The Egyptians made tools for the big jobs, such as building pyramids. They also made tools, such as saws, that they used in carpentry.

The Step Pyramid of King Djoser can be found at Saqqara, just south of Cairo. It is said to look like a stairway to heaven at certain times of the day. The all-stone pyramid is about 200 feet (61 m) high.

The Great Pyramids of Egypt

The ancient Egyptians believed in eternal life. To protect and preserve the bodies and the possessions of their kings, they created huge tombs of stone, called pyramids. The first pyramid was built around 2600 B.C., for King Djoser. This pyramid was named the Step Pyramid for its series of giant steps made from many smaller pieces of rock. Later the Egyptians invented a better method of construction that used larger blocks. These new pyramids had smooth sides. Each had a rectangular base and four flat sides that met in a point at the top. Some of these pyramids still stand at Giza, outside the ancient city of Memphis.

The ancient Egyptians relied on the yearly flooding of the Nile River to provide water for their farms. As the population grew, however, so did the number of farms. New farms were established beyond the floodwater area. The Egyptians developed an irrigation system that brought water to land not reached by the river's flooding. Using wooden hoes, workers dug pits in the ground to trap the floodwaters. They dug canals to carry the water to dry land. They built dikes, or walls of mud, that kept water from flowing to places it was not meant to go. As a result, farmers were able to grow several crops per season.

The water and rich soil from the Nile enabled plentiful harvests. An ancient Egyptian uses a sickle, or curved cutting blade, to harvest grain in this tomb painting. Sickles were fitted with sharp pieces of stone that cut like saw teeth.

Ancient Egyptians had an advanced irrigation system that allowed them to bring the Nile's water to their farms.

By 3000 B.C., the Egyptians had developed boats that were steered by oarsmen.

This fresco is from the tomb of Senefer, an important general in the 1450s B.C., after boats with sails had been invented.

Making Strides in Transportation

The first boats developed by the Egyptians were rafts. Rafts were made from papyrus stalks that were tied together. They were used to transport food and goods on the Nile. The rafts did not have sails. They were pushed along by the river's currents. By 2900 B.C., the Egyptians had improved the technology of shipbuilding. They invented sails that caught the wind and moved boats quickly through the water. Builders had also begun to make boats from wood. These were larger and sturdier than papyrus rafts. They enabled the Egyptians to transport heavy stone blocks for building. Wooden boats were strong enough to cross oceans in times of war.

The Egyptian Calendar

The Egyptians used the flood cycle of the Nile to measure time. Around 2800 B.C., they realized that the Nile flooded about every 365 days. They invented a calendar based on this cycle. The calendar was useful. Farmers could irrigate their land most effectively if they knew when to expect the floodwaters. The Egyptians divided their calendar into 12 months because they knew of the 12 cycles of change in the Moon's appearance. They grouped the 12 months into three seasons. Spring was when the Nile flooded. Winter was when land that had been underwater began to reappear. Summer marked the return of the dry period.

This is a papyrus copy of the ceiling of an Egyptian temple. It represents the Egyptian calendar year and shows how the year was divided.

The water clock was marked on the inside so that the Egyptians could tell how much time had passed. The water dripped into a pot below (not shown) through a small hole in the bottom of this pot.

The Invention of Clocks

The ancient Egyptians came up with some inventive ways to track time. One such invention was the sundial. This was a stick placed in the ground with a circle of numbers around it. The Sun moving overhead would create a shadow on the sundial, indicating which hour of the day it was. To measure time both day and night, they came up with the water clock. This consisted of a pot with a hole in the bottom, and another pot attached below. They would fill the top pot with water. As the water emptied into the lower pot, the Egyptians could tell how much time had passed by looking at the markings on the inside of the top pot.

Advances in Medicine

The Egyptians made some important medical discoveries. They found that medicines could be made from certain plants to treat patients. They developed various methods to treat wounds, such as using splints to set broken bones. The splints were made from wood and padded with cloth. Egyptian doctors found that washing their hands and heating their instruments with fire before surgery reduced infections in patients. The tools they used in medicine included sharp knives, lances, and scissors. For religious reasons, Egyptians did not study the bodies of dead people to gain medical knowledge. Advances in medicine were limited as a result.

A knife such as this was used to prepare Egyptian bodies for burial. Some of the body's internal organs needed to be removed.

Ancient Egyptian doctors used surgical instruments made from bronze, such as the ones shown here. These instruments were also used to prepare bodies for burial. The Egyptians often buried such tools with the dead in their tombs.

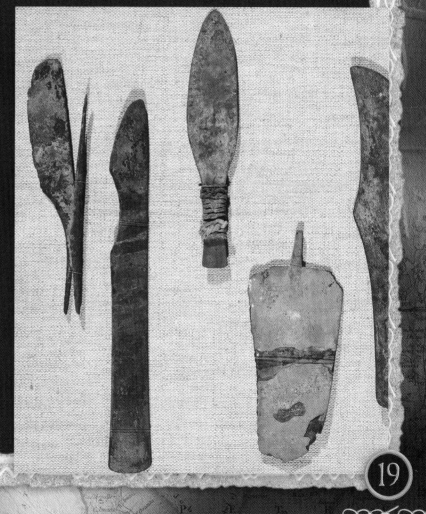

This relief from an Egyptian tomb shows workers gathering papyrus along the banks of the Nile. One of the most popular uses for papyrus was to make paper.

This limestone relief shows two scribes writing on papyrus. Scribes were the only people who could write in ancient Egypt.

Ancient Egyptians wrote in hieroglyphs with brushes made from plant stems. They dipped their brushes in ink, which was made from plant gum and water.

Writing It All Down

The Egyptians invented one of the world's first writing systems. Scholars, or educated people, wrote with picture symbols called hieroglyphs, which were developed so that kings could keep track of their land and livestock. Hieroglyphs were carved onto the walls of temples and tombs or were written on papyrus paper, also invented by the Egyptians. They made the paper from the stalks of the papyrus plant. They glued the stalks together with water and plant sap and then let it dry. These inventions allowed the Egyptians to record the events of their lives and scientific discoveries. Surviving hieroglyphs teach us much about the inventions of the Egyptians.

Building Better Weapons

In early Egypt, there were few wars. Weapons were therefore simple. Egyptians used weapons made from wood to protect themselves. However, after Egypt was attacked by the Hyksos in 1674 B.C., the Egyptians had to develop more advanced weapons. From their attackers, they learned how to make bronze weapons. They also learned how to build chariots. The Hyksos chariots were two-wheeled platforms pulled by horses. The Egyptians improved upon the chariot's design by lightening the horses' loads, freeing them to run faster. Egypt became a stronger civilization because of its many advances in technology.

Glossary

basalt (buh-SALT) A hard, dark-colored rock.

chisels (CHIH-zulz) Sharp tools used to cut or shape wood or stone.

cycle (SY-kul) A course of events that happens in the same order over and over.

developed (dih-VEH-lupt) Worked out in great detail.

fresco (FRES-koh) A painting done on wet plaster. Plaster is a mix of lime, sand, and water that hardens as it dries.

hieroglyphs (HY-ruh-glifs) A picture or symbol that stands for a word, word, a sound, or an idea.

Hyksos (HIK-sohs) A people who attacked Egypt and ruled it during the sixteenth and the seventeenth centuries B.C.

infections (in-FEK-shunz) Sicknesses caused by germs.

irrigation (ih-rih-GAY-shun) The carrying of water to land through ditches or pipes.

papyrus (puh-PY-rus) A tall plant that once flourished along the Nile River in Egypt.

pyramids (PEER-uh-midz) Large, stone structures with square bottoms and triangular sides that meet at a point on top.

rafts (RAFTS) Flat boats.

surgery (SER-juh-ree) An operation performed by a doctor.

surviving (sur-VYV-ing) Continuing to exist.

tombs (TOOMZ) Graves.

transport (TRANZ-port) To move something from one place to another.

Index

B
bronze, 6, 22

C
calendar, 5, 14
canals, 10
chariot(s), 22
chisels, 6

D
dikes, 10
Djoser, king of
    Egypt, 9

G
Giza, Egypt, 9

H
hieroglyphs, 21
hoes, 10
Hyksos, 22

I
irrigation system, 5,
    10

M
medicines, 18

N
Nile River, 5–6,
    10, 13–14

P
papyrus, 13, 21
pyramids, 5–6, 9

R
rafts, 13

S
shipbuilding, 13
Step Pyramid, 9
sundial, 17
surgery, 18

Primary Sources

Cover. Workmen carrying building materials. Detail of a wall painting in the tomb of Rekhmire, vizier under the pharaohs Thutmosis III and Amenhophis II. Eighteenth Dynasty. **Inset.** Ivory and flint knife. Pre-dynastic era. **Page 4.** Ship transporting goods. Relief from mastaba of Ipy. Circa 2494–2345 B.C. **Page 7.** Carpenters at work. Detail of a wall painting. Tomb of Rekhmire, vizier under Pharaohs Thutmose III and Amenophis II. Cemetery of Sheik Abd al-Qurnah. Circa 1504–1425 B.C. Thebes, Egypt. **Page 11. Top.** Sennedjem and his wife harvesting wheat in the fields of Yaru. Fresco. Tomb of Sennedjem, servant in the Place of Truth. Deir el-Medineh. Circa 1320–1200 B.C. **Page 12.** Boat sailing along the Nile. Fresco. Tomb of Senefer. Mayor of Thebes and general of Pharaoh Amenhotep II. 1450–1425 B.C. Valley of the Nobles. Qurna, Egypt. **Inset.** Hunters in papyrus reed boats with captured birds in baskets and lotus blossoms. Relief. Egyptian Museum. Cairo, Egypt. **Page 15.** Copy on papyrus of the Zodiac ceiling in the Temple of Hathor in Dendera, Egypt. Shows the four cardinal points of the zodiac (women in white) and 36 decans (10-day divisions of the 360-day Egyptian year). **Page 16.** Ancient Egyptian water clock. Reproduction of alabaster original. Cone is marked with 10 columns of 12 indentations on interior to tell time as water seeped from the small hole in bottom. Pharaonic Village. Cairo, Egypt. **Page 19.** Egyptian bronze surgical instruments. Musée d'Histoire de la Medicine, Paris, France. **Inset.** Embalmer's knife with Anubis, god of embalming, on the papyrus-shaped handle. Minmesout, the embalmer's name, is on the blade. 1554–1196 B.C.

Web Sites

Due to the changing nature of Internet links, PowerKids Press has developed an online list of Web sites related to the subject of this book. This site is updated regularly. Please use this link to access the list:
www.powerkidslinks.com/psaciv/techegy/